THE SOLAR S

JUPITER

A MyReportLinks.com Book

STEPHEN FEINSTEIN

MyReportLinks.com Books

an imprint of

 Enslow Publishers, Inc.

Box 398, 40 Industrial Road
Berkeley Heights, NJ 07922
USA

MyReportLinks.com Books, an imprint of Enslow Publishers, Inc. MyReportLinks® is a registered trademark of Enslow Publishers, Inc.

Library of Congress Cataloging-in-Publication Data

Feinstein, Stephen.
  Jupiter / Stephen Feinstein.
      p. cm. — (The solar system)
  Includes bibliographical references and index.
  ISBN 0-7660-5303-2
  1. Jupiter (Planet)—Juvenile literature. I. Title. II. Solar system (Berkeley Heights, N.J.)
  QB661.F45 2005
  523.45—dc22
                                    2004019461

Printed in the United States of America

10 9 8 7 6 5 4 3 2 1

To Our Readers:
Through the purchase of this book, you and your library gain access to the Report Links that specifically back up this book.
The Publisher will provide access to the Report Links that back up this book and will keep these Report Links up to date on **www.myreportlinks.com** for five years from the book's first publication date.
We have done our best to make sure all Internet addresses in this book were active and appropriate when we went to press. However, the author and the Publisher have no control over, and assume no liability for, the material available on those Internet sites or on other Web sites they may link to.
The usage of the MyReportLinks.com Books Web site is subject to the terms and conditions stated on the Usage Policy Statement on **www.myreportlinks.com**.
A password may be required to access the Report Links that back up this book. The password is found on the bottom of page 4 of this book.
Any comments or suggestions can be sent by e-mail to comments@myreportlinks.com or to the address on the back cover.

Photo Credits: Clipart.com, p. 13; Cornell University, p. 28; Lunar and Planetary Institute, pp. 19, 20; MyReportLinks.com Books, p. 4; National Aeronautics and Space Administration (NASA), 3, 9, 10, 14, 22, 23, 24, 27, 29, 32, 33, 34, 37, 39, 41, 43; National Air and Space Museum, p. 30; Photos.com, pp. 3, 9; Space Flight Now.com, p. 44; Windows to the Universe, pp. 11, 17.

Note: Some NASA photos were only available in a low-resolution format.

Cover Photo: National Aeronautics and Space Administration.

MyReportLinks.com Books
Great Books, Great Links, Great for Research!

The Internet sites listed on the next four pages can save you hours of research time. These Internet sites—we call them "Report Links"—are constantly changing, but we keep them up to date on our Web site.

Give it a try! Type http://www.myreportlinks.com into your browser, click on the series title, then the book title, and scroll down to the Report Links listed for this book.

The Report Links will bring you to great source documents, photographs, and illustrations. MyReportLinks.com Books save you time, feature Report Links that are kept up to date, and make report writing easier than ever!

Please see "To Our Readers" on the copyright page for important information about this book, the MyReportLinks.com Web site, and the Report Links that back up this book.

Please enter **PJU1502** if asked for a password.

Report Links

 The Internet sites described below can be accessed at
http://www.myreportlinks.com

*EDITOR'S CHOICE

▶**Jupiter: Your Travel Guide to the Solar System**
Learn about Jupiter, the largest planet in the solar system, at this BBC
site. Information about how long it takes to get to Jupiter and what you
will see when you get there is included.

*EDITOR'S CHOICE

▶**Galileo: Journey to Jupiter**
After fourteen years of studying Jupiter's atmosphere, the *Galileo*
mission ended in September 2003. This site provides information
on the mission as well as what it has discovered about Jupiter.

*EDITOR'S CHOICE

▶**Welcome to the Planets: Jupiter**
Take an online photographic tour of Jupiter at this NASA site. Visit the
Great Red Spot, see white clouds and lightning storms, and view Jupiter
in its beautiful natural colors.

*EDITOR'S CHOICE

▶**Windows to the Universe: Jupiter**
This site has information on Jupiter's atmosphere, magnetosphere, moons,
space missions, mythology, and other planetary facts and statistics. The
material is also available in Spanish.

*EDITOR'S CHOICE

▶**Solar System Exploration: Jupiter**
This NASA site offers a comprehensive overview of Jupiter, the largest
planet in our solar system. You will find a picture gallery as well as
information on Jupiter's moons, rings, and much more.

*EDITOR'S CHOICE

▶**The Satellites of Jupiter**
For almost three centuries following their discovery by Galileo in 1610,
it was believed that Jupiter only had four moons, or satellites. The number
totaled sixty-three in 2002. Find out more about the Galilean satellites
at this site.

Any comments? Contact us: **comments@myreportlinks.com**   5

		STOP					
Back	Forward	Stop	Review	Home	Explore	Favorites	History

Report Links

The Internet sites described below can be accessed at
http://www.myreportlinks.com

▶**Cassini's First Look at Jupiter**

A deep space probe took an extensive number of photographs of Jupiter that revealed
ammonia ice particles, huge storms, swirling clouds, and the famous Great Red Spot.
Learn more about the Cassini mission at this Web site.

▶**A Close Encounter With Jupiter**

In March 2004, Jupiter and Earth came within 400 million miles of each other. On this
site, learn more about this "close encounter."

▶**Comet Shoemaker-Levy 9 Collision With Jupiter**

For the first time in history, scientists were able to predict and detect the impact of
one solar system body on another—in this case, Comet Shoemaker-Levy 9's impact
of Jupiter. This NASA site tells the story of the Shoemakers and David Levy, the
scientists who predicted this event.

▶**Comet Shoemaker-Levy 9 Collision With Jupiter (Another Look)**

For the first time, the collision of two objects in space was viewed and monitored
during the week of July 16–22, 1994. Scientists and astronomers around the world
watched as a comet smashed into Jupiter. This site offers images of the collision.

▶**Exploring the Planets: Jupiter**

This is the National Air and Space Museum site for the planet Jupiter. Learn about
Jupiter's moons, radiation belts, magnetic field, and atmosphere. See some photographs
of the biggest planet of all.

▶**Future Jupiter Exploration on the Drawing Boards**

The Galileo mission found strong evidence for a large subsurface ocean on Jupiter's
moon Europa. This site explores NASA's plan to develop a fleet of nuclear-powered
spacecraft to orbit Jupiter's moons in search of water.

▶**Galileo**

NASA's space science library resources for the Galileo mission to Jupiter are available
at this Web site. You will find images, data, news, and instructional materials about
the planet.

▶**Galileo Galilei (1564–1642)**

In 1610, Galileo discovered the four largest moons of Jupiter—Io, Europa, Ganymede,
and Callisto—using a telescope he had made himself. Learn more about the life of this
mathematician and astronomer at this BBC Web site.

Report Links

The Internet sites described below can be accessed at http://www.myreportlinks.com

▶ Galileo Legacy Site

Jupiter is larger than all the other planets combined and is made primarily of hydrogen and helium. This site offers some great educational resources and tries to solve some of Jupiter's mysteries.

▶ The Galileo Project: Satellites of Jupiter

Learn about Jupiter's moons from the Galileo Project. View a page from Galileo's original manuscript describing his observations of the planet's moons, and read about how other moons were discovered.

▶ Galileo Project Information

The Galileo mission to Jupiter had specific scientific goals and objectives attached to the project when it was launched. From this site, learn what scientists have discovered about the planet.

▶ Great Images in NASA: Planet Jupiter

You can download great images of Jupiter from this NASA Web site. Click on the "more information" links for a more detailed description of each image.

▶ Jupiter

Learn about Jupiter and its moons from this comprehensive Web site. View photographs of the planet and charts of data. Information on Jupiter's Great Red Spot and ring system are also included.

▶ Jupiter's Ring System

Unlike Saturn's intricate and complex ring patterns, Jupiter has a faint ring system that is probably composed of dust particles. At this site, learn about the ring system through animations and other images.

▶ *A Meeting With the Universe*

Space exploration has changed the way we see and understand Earth. Learn why by reading the complete text of *A Meeting With the Universe,* a book written by NASA scientists for nonscientific readers, available on this Web site.

▶ National Maritime Museum: Jupiter

The National Maritime Museum in London has compiled some important material on Jupiter. On this site you will find information on the planet's appearance, satellites, and magnetic atmosphere, as well as information on the comet that crashed into it. Follow the links to continue the article.

Report Links

The Internet sites described below can be accessed at http://www.myreportlinks.com

▶National Weather Service Forecast Office: Jupiter

This NOAA site has an overview of Jupiter and its weather conditions and atmosphere. Some quick facts and a note on the Shoemaker-Levy 9 comet collision are also included.

▶Nineplanets.org: Jupiter

This Web site provides a comprehensive overview of the planet Jupiter. Learn about this gas giant's rings and satellites. Links to other important information are included.

▶NSSDC Photo Gallery: Jupiter

On this Web site from NASA, you can view images of Jupiter, its Great Red Spot, and its moons.

▶The Planet Jupiter

This site provides lots of facts about Jupiter, including descriptions of its surface features, cloud layers, and more.

▶The Solar System

This Liverpool Museum site provides an information page on each planet in the solar system, as well as facts on comets, asteroids, and meteorites. Learn more about Jupiter and its Great Red Spot.

▶Solar System Bodies: Jupiter

Learn about the gas planet Jupiter from this site. A statistical profile is included, as well as information on its satellites and rings. Take a look at the diagram of the planet's moons.

▶Super-Thunderstorms on Jupiter

Jupiter has long storms with tremendous winds, rain, and oversized lightning bolts. This site explains how conditions on the planet make for turbulent weather.

▶Tour the Solar System and Beyond: Jupiter

NASA has launched many missions to the planet Jupiter, including the Voyager, Pioneer, and Galileo missions. Each has returned a great deal of information to scientists on Earth. At this site, learn more about these missions.

Jupiter Facts

Age
About 4.5 billion years

Diameter at Equator
88,793 miles (142,898 kilometers)

Composition
Giant ball of gas with a dense, rocky core

Average Distance From the Sun
About 484 million miles (779 million kilometers)

Distance From Earth
Minimum: About 391 million miles (629 million kilometers)
Maximum: About 577 million miles (929 million kilometers)

Orbital Period (year, in Earth years)
11.86 years

Rotational Period (day, in Earth hours)
9.9 hours

Mass
318 times as massive as Earth

Density
Less than one fourth that of Earth

Atmosphere
86 percent hydrogen and 14 percent helium, with trace amounts of ammonia, phosphorus, water vapor, and methane

Average Temperature
Top of clouds: −234°F (−148°C)

Number of moons
Sixty-three

The Biggest Planet

Jupiter, the fifth planet from the Sun, is the largest planet in the solar system. It was formed about 4.5 billion years ago at the same time as the other planets in the Sun's family. While Earth and the other "terrestrial" or Earth-like inner planets—Mercury, Venus, and Mars—are solid objects composed mainly of rock and metal, Jupiter does not have a solid surface. It is a giant ball of gas and may have a dense core made of solid rock or metal—or, according to some scientists, no core at all.

With the exception of Pluto, Jupiter and the other outer planets of the solar system—Saturn, Neptune, and Uranus—are all gas giants. And Jupiter is a giant among giants, with a diameter at its equator of 88,793 miles (142,898 kilometers). It is more than three times as massive as Saturn, the next largest planet. Earth, with a diameter of 7,926 miles (12,753 kilometers), is a tiny planet compared to Jupiter. More than thirteen hundred Earths could fit inside Jupiter.

▶ Jupiter, King of the Gods

For thousands of years, most people believed that all of the visible objects in the sky—the

Jupiter is by far the largest planet in the solar system. Excluding the Sun, this gas giant contains approximately 71 percent of all the material in the solar system.

Jupiter - Microsoft Internet Explorer

File Edit View Favorites Tools Help

Address http://www.windows.ucar.edu/tour/link=/mythology/Definitions_gods/Jupiter_def.html

Windows to the Universe

Beginner Intermediate Advanced

Spanish
English

Jupiter

In Roman mythology, Jupiter was the king of heaven and Earth and of all the Olympian gods. He was also known as the god of justice. He was named king of the gods in the special meeting that followed his overthrow of the god Saturn and the Titans.

Jupiter granted Neptune dominion over the Sea, and his other brother Pluto dominion over the underworld. Jupiter's wife was Juno, who was very jealous of the attention that he paid to other goddesses and women.

Done   Internet

▲ *The planet Jupiter was named for the king of the gods in Roman mythology.*

Sun, Moon, stars, and planets—revolved around Earth. People in ancient times also believed that the heavenly bodies were either gods or associated with the gods. Many believed that the stars and planets spent their days in the Underworld and the Sun disappeared into the Underworld each night.

The ancient Babylonians believed that Jupiter was a wandering star placed in the heavens by a god to watch over the night sky. They named it after their god Marduk. The ancient Greeks named the planet after Zeus, the king of the gods in Greek mythology. They had observed that the planet, which is visible for most of the year, was the third brightest object (after the Moon and Venus) in the night sky. Its brilliance suggested that the planet was a source of great power in the heavens.

Like the Greeks, the Romans observed that the planet occupied a dominant position in the heavens and named it after Jupiter, king of the Roman gods. Jupiter, the Roman version of Zeus, was believed to have the power to control the lives of individual humans, making sure they lived according to their fate. Jupiter was also thought to rule the sky and control the weather on Earth. Using a thunderbolt as a weapon, Jupiter had the power to hurl storms at Earth.

Another name for Jupiter is Jove. Today, the adjective *Jovian* is used to describe anything associated with Jupiter, such as the Jovian atmosphere, Jovian moons, and Jovian system, a term used to describe Jupiter and its many satellites. The largest planets are also sometimes referred to as Jovian planets.

An Ancient View of the World

The first people to make systematic studies of the heavens believed that an Earth which did not move was the center of the universe. This view is known as the geocentric theory, and it was supported by common-sense observations. Nobody could feel or see the movements of Earth, so they did not know that it rotated on an axis or revolved around the Sun. But everyone could see that the Sun rose in the east, made a trip across the sky, and then set in the west. The movements of the Moon, planets, and stars in the heavens were also evident.

One ancient Greek astronomer who came to a completely different conclusion was Aristarchus of Samos. Aristarchus became convinced that the Sun was a much larger body than Earth and that the Sun was at the center of the solar system. According to Aristarchus' heliocentric, or Sun-centered, theory, all the planets including Earth revolved around the Sun. Most people at the time ignored Aristarchus' ideas because they seemed to go against common sense. Claudius Ptolemy, a Greek astronomer of the second century A.D., wrote a complex, detailed description of a geocentric universe that reinforced the common

view. The Earth-centered theory remained unchallenged for almost fifteen hundred years.

An Early Look at Jupiter

In 1543, the Polish astronomer Nicolaus Copernicus published *On the Revolutions of the Celestial Spheres.* Copernicus was aware of the ideas of Aristarchus, and after studying the heavens, he found himself agreeing with the ancient Greek astronomer. Copernicus made a strong argument for the heliocentric theory, showing it to be simpler than the geocentric theory. As later scientists added evidence to the heliocentric theory, it eventually became accepted fact that Earth and the other planets revolved around the Sun.

On January 7, 1610, the Italian astronomer Galileo Galilei became the first person to look at Jupiter through a telescope. He observed the planet as a disk and also was able to see the four largest satellites, or moons, of Jupiter—Io, Europa, Ganymede, and Callisto. At first, Galileo was not sure what these four objects were. He wrote, "They aroused my curiosity somewhat by appearing to lie in an exact straight line

On January 7, 1610, Galileo Galilei was the first person to view Jupiter through a telescope. The Italian astronomer was also the first to identify Io, Europa, Ganymede, and Callisto, now known as the Galilean moons of Jupiter.

◁ *This image of the Jovian system combines the huge storm known as the Great Red Spot and the Galilean moons.*

parallel to the ecliptic [the Sun's annual path], and by their being more splendid than others of their size."[1] Galileo studied the four satellites for a week. He then wrote that "the revolutions are swifter in those planets [moons] which describe smaller circles around Jupiter, since the stars [moons] closest to Jupiter are usually seen to the east when on the previous day they appeared to the west, and vice versa."[2] When he realized that the small starlike objects he observed actually revolved around Jupiter, Galileo believed his discovery would strengthen the support for the heliocentric ideas of Copernicus.[3] People would now have to acknowledge that not all heavenly bodies revolved around Earth.

Galileo's observations of Jupiter's moons also destroyed another long-standing belief. For centuries, people thought that Earth could not possibly revolve around the Sun because if it did, it would lose its Moon. Since astronomers agreed that Jupiter moved and its moons stayed with it, there was no reason why a moving Earth should lose its Moon.

As more powerful telescopes became available, astronomers were able to learn much more about Jupiter and the other planets. In 1665, the Italian astronomer Giovanni Domenico Cassini observed Jupiter's stripes—bands of clouds moving around the planet. He also observed the Great Red Spot, a huge storm on

Jupiter that has raged for hundreds of years. The Great Red Spot may have been seen a year earlier by the English astronomer and physicist Robert Hooke. By studying the movements of the planets, Cassini calculated the distances between them and found that Jupiter is five times farther from the Sun than Earth is.

Once the distances were known, scientists were able to determine Jupiter's size. By observing the effect of Jupiter's gravity on its moons, they were also able to determine Jupiter's mass, the amount of matter or material in the planet. Jupiter's mass is about 318 times Earth's mass. Astronomers then determined that Jupiter's density was only about one fourth that of Earth, even though the planet's volume was more than a thousand times the volume of Earth. By the end of the eighteenth century, it had become clear to astronomers that Jupiter was a very different sort of planet than Earth.

Stronger Telescopes, More Moons

In the nineteenth century, larger and stronger telescopes with mirrors in place of lenses allowed astronomers to see much more of Jupiter. They were able to observe many more details in Jupiter's clouds. Amalthea, a fifth moon of Jupiter, was discovered in 1892 by Edward E. Barnard in California. By the 1930s, astronomers began using instruments called spectrometers to analyze the chemical composition of Jupiter's atmosphere. Methane and ammonia were discovered in Jupiter's atmosphere in 1932. In the 1950s, the American astronomer Gerard Kuiper, considered the father of modern planetary science, calculated the amount and proportions of methane and ammonia in Jupiter's atmosphere. In 1955, B. F. Burke and K. L. Franklin, radio astronomers at the Carnegie Institution in Washington, D.C., detected radio waves from Jupiter, which came from the planet's strong magnetic field. The next great leap forward in our knowledge of Jupiter would come with the launching of unmanned space probes.

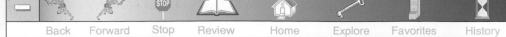
Chapter 2 ▶

A Giant Ball of Gas

The giant ball of gas known as Jupiter is the second largest body in the solar system after the Sun. It is so huge that, excluding the Sun, it contains about 71 percent of all the material in the solar system. All of the other planets can fit inside Jupiter.

Jupiter's distance from Earth varies from 391 million miles (629 million kilometers) to 577 million miles (929 million kilometers). Even though it is so far from Earth, Jupiter has an effect on our own planet and others. Scientists believe that Jupiter's gravity shielded Earth from most of the asteroids and comets that would have struck our planet otherwise.[1] Jupiter's gravity is 2.36 times Earth's gravity. If Jupiter had a solid surface and you were able to stand on it, you would weigh almost two and a half times as much as you weigh on Earth.

▶ How Jupiter Was Formed

Scientists believe that the Sun and the planets of the solar system formed about 4.5 billion years ago. They think that gravitational forces pulled together hydrogen and helium gas and dust particles floating in the space between the stars into a spinning disk. According to this theory, the Sun formed first at the center of the disk, and then the planets formed out of dust and clumps of rocky debris circling the Sun.

The inner part of the disk closest to the Sun was hot, and Earth and the other rocky and metallic inner planets of the solar system formed here. Farther out from the Sun in a much colder region of the disk, lumps of ice and frozen gases formed other bodies. Hydrogen and helium gases blown outward by the Sun

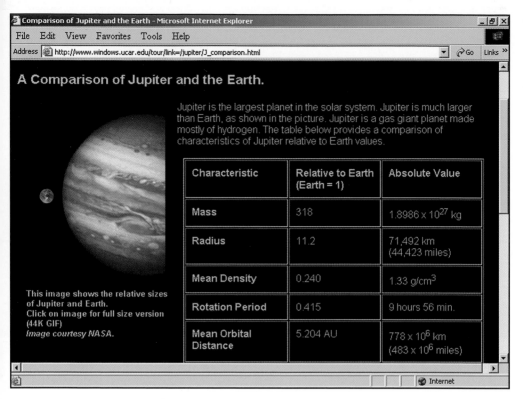

File   Edit   View   Favorites   Tools   Help

Address http://www.windows.ucar.edu/tour/link=/jupiter/J_comparison.html ▼ ⬀ Go | Links »

A Comparison of Jupiter and the Earth.

Jupiter is the largest planet in the solar system. Jupiter is much larger than Earth, as shown in the picture. Jupiter is a gas giant planet made mostly of hydrogen. The table below provides a comparison of characteristics of Jupiter relative to Earth values.

Characteristic	Relative to Earth (Earth = 1)	Absolute Value
Mass	318	1.8986×10^{27} kg
Radius	11.2	71,492 km (44,423 miles)
Mean Density	0.240	1.33 g/cm^3
Rotation Period	0.415	9 hours 56 min.
Mean Orbital Distance	5.204 AU	778×10^6 km (483×10^6 miles)

This image shows the relative sizes of Jupiter and Earth.
Click on image for full size version (44K GIF)
Image courtesy NASA.

Internet

▲ Perhaps the most obvious difference between Jupiter and our own planet is size: Over thirteen hundred Earths could fit inside Jupiter.

from the inner part of the solar system added to the huge gas cloud around these bodies. The gravitational pull of these young outer planets attracted more and more gases, and they continued to grow larger. Jupiter became the largest planet because it was situated in the thickest part of the gas cloud and it attracted the most gas.

▶ Planet or Star?

Most of the planets of the solar system shine by reflected sunlight. But unlike our own planet, Jupiter is a giant glowing globe with its own internal source of heat. It gives off more than one and a half times as much energy as it receives from the Sun. So

where does all of this energy come from? Many scientists believe that when Jupiter formed, it was larger than it is today. Jupiter shrank and built up heat energy while it contracted. Gravitational energy was converted to heat as particles of matter fell inward due to gravity and collided with each other. Jupiter is still contracting, at the rate of about one inch a year. There is so much leftover heat still inside Jupiter that the planet continues to pump out more energy than it receives.

Jupiter is very similar to the Sun in some ways. Both bodies have their own internal energy source and have extremely hot interiors, and both are mostly made up of hydrogen, as are most stars. Helium is the second most abundant element in both bodies. And Jupiter and the Sun both have small amounts of carbon, oxygen, and nitrogen in their outer atmospheres. So why is Jupiter a planet and not a star? According to scientists, the Sun became hotter inside than Jupiter, hot enough to trigger the process that makes it shine. This process, known as thermonuclear fusion, occurred in the Sun and not in Jupiter because the Sun has one thousand times the mass of Jupiter, so its gravity can produce the immense temperature and pressure needed for a nuclear reaction to occur. Some astronomers think that if Jupiter had been only between fifty and eighty times as massive as it is now, it might have become a star.[2] Its core temperature and pressure would have been high enough to begin this process. So although Jupiter is a planet, some astronomers think of it as a star that did not quite make it, or a "substar."

▶ Jupiter's Structure

Jupiter is made up of several layers. The planet is completely shrouded in the clouds of its outermost atmospheric layer. The atmosphere is about 86 percent hydrogen and 14 percent helium, with trace amounts of ammonia, phosphorus, water vapor, and methane. Jupiter's rapid rotation causes clouds in its atmosphere to be drawn into dark and light bands or stripes. Scientists refer

to the dark bands as belts and the light bands as zones. These belts and zones run parallel to Jupiter's equator.

The dark and light bands of clouds, mainly reddish and white, circle the planet. Orange, blue, brown, and yellow tones can also be seen in these clouds. Astronomers are not sure what causes the colors in Jupiter's clouds. Some think they could be the result of clear gases in the atmosphere interacting with ultraviolet radiation from the Sun, coloring the clear gases. The red color might also be caused by lightning, extreme temperature variations, the breakdown of gas molecules to produce sulfur or phosphorous compounds, or gas molecules drawn up by storms from lower parts of the atmosphere.

The atmosphere consists of three layers. The top layer is made of clouds of ammonia ice crystals. The temperature at the top of

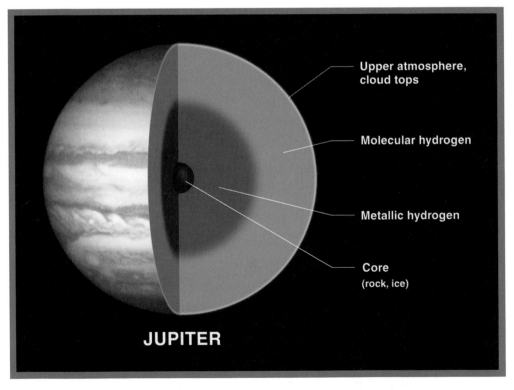

JUPITER

▲ Jupiter is a planet whose "surface" is made up of mostly hydrogen and helium, while its dense core—if it has one—may be mostly rock and ice.

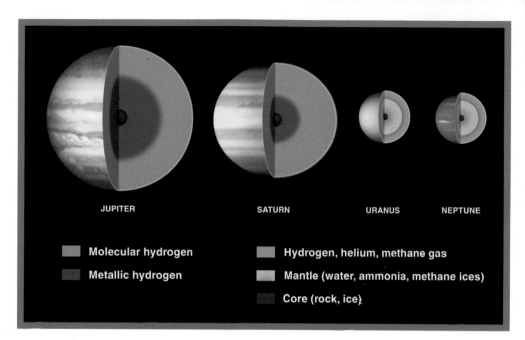

JUPITER   SATURN   URANUS   NEPTUNE

Molecular hydrogen	Hydrogen, helium, methane gas
Metallic hydrogen	Mantle (water, ammonia, methane ices)
	Core (rock, ice)

▲ *This diagram compares the compositions of the Jovian planets: Jupiter, Saturn, Uranus, and Neptune.*

this cloud layer is very cold, averaging about −234°F (−148°C). A middle layer consists of crystals of ammonia and hydrogen sulfide. The lowest layer may be warm enough to consist of clouds of water or water ice.

▶ Heavy Pressure, High Temperatures

The temperatures and pressure inside Jupiter increase with depth. Increasing pressure and higher temperatures cause the hydrogen gas to change form. Beneath the atmosphere, at a depth of about 600 miles (965 kilometers), is a layer of liquid hydrogen that covers most of Jupiter. Deeper down, the tremendous pressures and temperatures as high as about 43,000°F (24,000°C) cause the liquid hydrogen to be squeezed into liquid metallic form. Beneath the layer of liquid metallic hydrogen is the planet's relatively small core (although Jupiter's core may be ten times the size of Earth).

For a long time, most scientists believed that Jupiter had a dense core made of solid (or possibly liquid) rock and metal, but recent findings have led many scientists to think otherwise. Some now believe that Jupiter has no core at all—that as Jupiter formed, the heaviest elements were broken up and spread out rather than collecting at the planet's center.

Stormy Weather

Jupiter's turbulent winds and ever-present storms constantly change the appearance of the clouds that surround the planet. Winds as high as 300 miles per hour (483 kilometers per hour) drive these cloud bands. The winds blow in different directions, so some bands move from west to east while others move from east to west. Huge whirlpools and eddies create wavy patterns that form along the edges of bands moving in different directions. White, red, and brown spots seen in Jupiter's atmosphere also indicate huge storms. Such storms gain energy by merging with and enclosing smaller eddies. Scientists believe that Jupiter's stormy weather is driven by the planet's internal store of heat.

Weather conditions in Jupiter's atmosphere live up to the Roman god's reputation as a creator of storms and hurler of thunderbolts. Water in Jupiter's lower atmosphere forms thunderclouds that generate huge bolts of lightning. Lightning ten thousand times more powerful than any lightning on Earth flashes between the clouds.

Jupiter's Great Red Spot

Jupiter's most noticeable feature is an enormous storm system in the planet's southern hemisphere known as the Great Red Spot. It is a gigantic shallow eddy, the largest of hundreds of different storms on Jupiter, and it acts like a continual hurricane. The Great Red Spot measures nearly 25,000 miles (40,225 kilometers) across, almost three times as wide as Earth. The huge storm whirls around at a speed of 250 miles per hour (402 kilometers per hour).

▲ Voyager 1 *captured this image of Jupiter's Great Red Spot and one of the planet's three famous white ovals. The Great Red Spot is an enormous storm that is believed to be at least three hundred years old while the while ovals are collections of clouds that were first seen in 1939.*

Astronomers have observed the Great Red Spot, the oldest known storm system in the solar system, for at least three hundred years.[3] How can a storm last so long? Scientists believe the Great Red Spot is partially driven by heat rising up from a lower part of the atmosphere directly beneath it. They have also seen that the Great Red Spot is caught between two belts of wind blowing past it in opposite directions, which keep the spot spinning.

Chapter 3 ▶

The Movements of Jupiter

Jupiter is much farther away from the Sun than Earth is. That is why it takes Jupiter 11.86 Earth years to complete one revolution around the Sun. The greater its distance from the Sun, the slower a planet moves along its orbital path. Not only does Jupiter have to travel a greater distance than Earth to complete its journey around the Sun, but it moves at a slower speed. So while Earth speeds along at an average velocity of 66,638 miles per hour

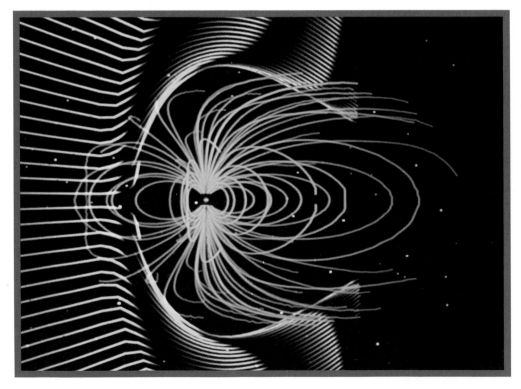

▲ Jupiter's magnetic field is more than ten times stronger than the magnetic field of our own planet.

(107,221 kilometers per hour), Jupiter moves at only 29,214 miles per hour (47,005 kilometers per hour).

Jupiter's Rapid Rotation

Like Earth and the other planets, Jupiter rotates on its axis as it moves along its orbit around the Sun. We know that it takes Earth about twenty-four hours, or one day, to rotate once on its axis. What we might be surprised to learn is that it takes giant Jupiter fewer than ten hours to complete one rotation as it spins faster than any other planet. It rotates so fast that a full day on Jupiter is less than half a day on Earth. Night and day on Jupiter each last for only about five hours.

A Bulging Middle

In 1692, astronomer Giovanni Cassini, who had been observing Jupiter through a telescope for many years, noticed that Jupiter's rate of rotation was faster at the planet's equator than at the higher latitudes, closer to the poles.[1] He learned this by tracking the movements of the markings in Jupiter's clouds, which cover the planet. Observations by many astronomers since then have shown that Jupiter's rate of rotation is

Jupiter Aurora HST • STIS • WFPC2
PRC98-04 • ST ScI OPO • January 7, 1998
J. Clarke (University of Michigan) and NASA

◄ *This image shows auroras, described by NASA as "brilliant curtains of light," at Jupiter's magnetic poles.*

about nine hours and fifty minutes near the equator and about nine hours and fifty-five minutes at higher latitudes.

The fact that Jupiter rotates faster near its middle has caused the planet to bulge outward at the equator. The unequal rates of rotation have also caused a slight flattening of the planet at its poles. Jupiter's rapid rotation also drives electrical currents in the liquid metallic hydrogen in the planet's interior. These electrical currents, in turn, generate Jupiter's powerful magnetic field.

Jupiter's Magnetosphere

Jupiter's magnetic field, the region where magnetic forces can be detected, is extremely powerful, much more powerful than Earth's. It extends into space millions of miles beyond Jupiter. This magnetic region, known as the magnetosphere, traps some of the particles of the solar wind, the stream of electromagnetic particles blowing outward from the Sun. When these particles enter Jupiter's atmosphere, they collide with gas molecules above Jupiter's polar regions and cause them to glow. A similar phenomenon called the aurora, or northern and southern lights, exists on Earth.

The Jovian System

Jupiter and its many satellites are known as the Jovian system. The giant planet and its moons and rings are like a miniature solar system in which Jupiter's gravity controls the motions of thousands of small objects. The number of known moons that revolve around Jupiter is sixty-three. Some scientists, however, think that the planet may actually have one hundred or more moons.

Jupiter's four largest moons—Io, Europa, Ganymede, and Callisto—are as large as planets. They are known as the Galilean satellites in honor of Galileo, the astronomer who discovered them in 1610. Each Galilean moon has unique qualities and features. There are also four small inner moons—Metis, Adrastea, Amalthea, and Thebe. Their diameters range in size from about 12 to 117 miles (19 to 188 kilometers). Amalthea was discovered in 1892, making it the fifth known moon of Jupiter. The other three inner moons were discovered in 1979 during the Voyager missions.

The other fifty-five Jovian moons are known as "irregulars." The irregulars, situated beyond the orbit of Callisto, follow elongated, tilted paths around Jupiter. Himalia, the largest of this group, has a diameter of 114 miles (183 kilometers). It was discovered in 1904 by the American astronomer Charles Dillon Perrine. The following year he discovered Elara. Pasiphae was discovered in 1908, Sinope in 1914, Lysithea and Carme in 1938, Ananke in 1951, and Leda in 1974. All of the other moons of Jupiter are very small, with diameters ranging in size from about 0.62 mile to 5.6 miles (1 to 9 kilometers). They were discovered between the years 2000 and 2004.

The irregulars fall into two separate groups. The inner group revolves around Jupiter at a distance of about 6.8 million miles (11 million kilometers). The outer group, about 12.4 million miles (20 million kilometers) from Jupiter, revolves around the planet in the opposite direction of the other satellites.[1] Scientists think that these irregular moons are what is left of the asteroids captured by Jupiter during the formation of the solar system. Those asteroids would have been smashed into pieces by debris hitting them, which left groups of fragments moving together around Jupiter.

About seventeen hundred small asteroids, known as the Trojan asteroids, also travel with Jupiter in its orbit. Grouped into two "clouds," they stay a fixed distance ahead of the planet and behind it. These asteroids came together at two of

Jupiter's four largest moons, Io, Europa, Ganymede, and Callisto, are shown in order of their distance from the planet.

▲ Jupiter's ring system is made up of dust from the planet's small inner satellites: Metis, Adraslea, Amalthea, and Thebe.

the points in space where the gravity of the Sun and the gravity of another planet (in this case, Jupiter) combine to keep an object from drifting away. These points are called the Lagrangian points. They are named for Joseph Louis Lagrange, the eighteenth-century mathematician who predicted their existence.

▶ Jupiter's Rings

In the seventeenth century, astronomers discovered that Saturn has rings, and for a long time, they thought that Saturn was the only planet to have these bands of small rocky or icy objects. But in 1977, scientists discovered that the planet Uranus has faint, narrow rings. Then in 1979, scientists confirmed that Jupiter, too, has rings. In 1984, rings were also discovered around the planet Neptune.

Jupiter's system of three rings is narrow and faint—not nearly as spectacular as the rings of Saturn. Two of Jupiter's inner moons, Metis and Adrastea, orbit near the ring system and keep it in place. The rings consist of a flat main ring, a cloudlike inner ring called the halo, and an outer ring. The outer ring, known as the gossamer ring, is actually two transparent rings.[2]

Jupiter's rings are made of dust particles. Astronomers believe the fine particles of dust are blasted off the surface of two of Jupiter's inner moons, Metis and Adrastea, when they are struck by meteoroids, fragments of comets and asteroids.[3] The creation of dust particles must be an ongoing process in order for the rings to continue to exist.

▶ Ganymede

Ganymede, with a diameter of 3,269 miles (5,260 kilometers), is the largest moon in the solar system. It is two-and-a-half times as large as Earth's Moon. It is even bigger than the planets Mercury and Pluto and is nearly as large as Mars. Ganymede orbits Jupiter at a distance of 664,900 miles (1,070,000 kilometers). Ganymede, like the other Galilean moons, has its own magnetic field. It also has a thin atmosphere of oxygen and ozone, produced by particles in Jupiter's magnetic field that bombarded water molecules in Ganymede's surface ice.

The Jovian moon Ganymede is the ▶ largest satellite in the solar system. It is even larger than the planets Mercury and Pluto.

Ganymede is made of roughly equal amounts of rock and ice. There are two types of surface—heavily cratered dark rocky areas and white icy areas with fewer impact craters. Two huge dark areas, Galileo Regio and Marius Regio, are the most prominent features on Ganymede's surface. Galileo Regio is about 2,000 miles (3,200 kilometers) across. Parallel curving grooves are visible in the light areas. Some grooves extend for thousands of miles across the surface. The grooves are probably the result of stretching and fracturing of the crust early in Ganymede's history. Ganymede's crust is about 47 miles (75 kilometers) thick. Beneath the crust is a mantle of rock and ice. At the center of Ganymede is a large rocky outer core, about the size of Earth's Moon, and a dense metallic inner core.

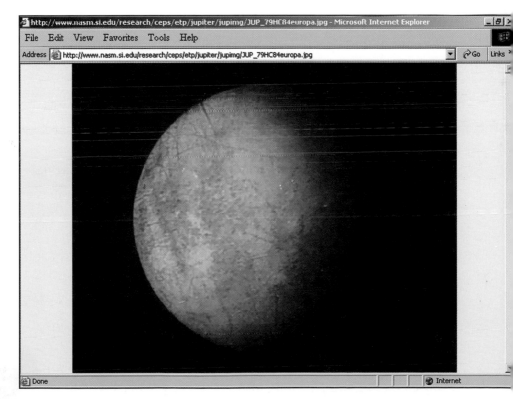

▲ This image of Europa features its dark and light colored lines. Scientists are eager to find out more about this strange moon, whose interior may contain a vast liquid ocean—making life there possible.

▶ Europa

Europa orbits Jupiter at a distance of 417,000 miles (670,900 kilometers). It is slightly smaller than Earth's Moon, with a diameter of 1,942 miles (3,125 kilometers). Europa has the smoothest surface of any planet or satellite in the solar system. Its flat, smooth surface is completely covered by water ice.

Because very few impact craters are visible on Europa, scientists believe that Europa's surface must have been flooded with water. The floodwaters would have filled in the craters and removed any evidence of asteroid impacts. But since Europa's surface has a temperature of −260°F (−162°C), where did the water come from? How can liquid water exist in such a frigid environment? Because of its closeness to Jupiter, Europa is affected by tidal forces caused by the massive planet's powerful gravitational field. Heat from the tidal forces causes a shifting and cracking of Europa's surface and heating of the interior. Indeed, astronomers believe that much of Europa's interior consists of a vast planetwide liquid ocean, an ocean bigger than all of Earth's oceans combined. They also speculate that Europa's subsurface ocean may be the best place in the solar system to search for extraterrestrial life. Beneath the ocean, Europa is believed to have a mantle of rock surrounding an iron core. In 1995, a thin atmosphere of oxygen was detected on Europa by the Hubble Space Telescope.

▶ Io

Io orbits Jupiter at a distance of 262,000 miles (421,558 kilometers). With a diameter of 2,257 miles (3,632 kilometers), Io is similar in size to Earth's Moon, although slightly larger. Io has mountains much taller than any found on Earth. Unlike the Moon, which is covered with impact craters, Io does not have a single crater. During its long history, Io has been just as much a target of impacting asteroids, meteorites, and comets as our own Moon was. But Io is also a place of volcanoes. In fact, with about

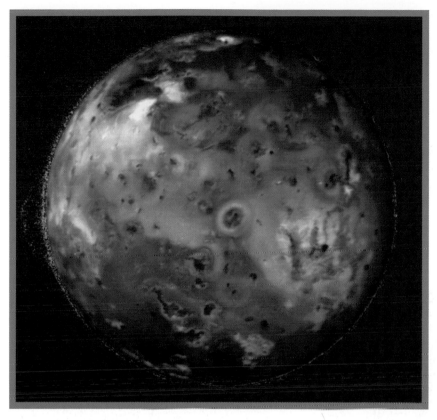

▲ *Io, whose surface is continually being changed by volcanic activity, is the closest of the Galilean moons to Jupiter.*

three hundred active volcanoes, Io is the most volcanically active body in the solar system. At least eighty of them are constantly erupting, spewing out lava all over Io's surface so that any impact craters soon disappear beneath the lava. Scientists have found that Io's volcanoes churn out 45,000 tons (41,000 metric tons) of lava every second.[4]

Io has an iron core surrounded by an interior of molten rock and a thin rocky crust. It has the hottest surface temperatures in the solar system except for the Sun. How does a Jovian satellite so far from the Sun in a frigid region of the solar system generate so much heat? Io is affected by Jupiter's powerful gravitational field

to a greater extent than the other Galilean satellites because it is closer to Jupiter. The huge planet creates tides in the body of Io. As Jupiter pulls at Io from one side, Io's other side feels the gravitational pull of Ganymede and Europa when those moons pass by. Io is caught in a tug-of-war, stretched and squeezed by immense tidal forces until its interior turns to molten rock.

Violent Volcanoes on Io

Io's volcanic activity is generated by the heating of the moon's interior. There is so much volcanic activity constantly occurring and so much material from the interior being deposited on the surface that the satellite almost seems to be turning itself inside out. Io's largest volcano is named Pele, after the Hawaiian goddess

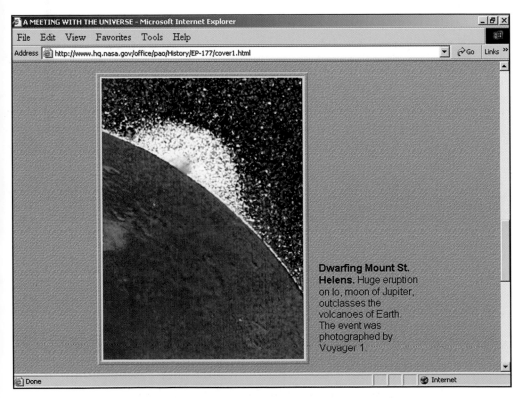

A MEETING WITH THE UNIVERSE - Microsoft Internet Explorer

File   Edit   View   Favorites   Tools   Help

Address http://www.hq.nasa.gov/office/pao/History/EP-177/cover1.html   Go   Links

Dwarfing Mount St. Helens. Huge eruption on Io, moon of Jupiter, outclasses the volcanoes of Earth. The event was photographed by Voyager 1.

Done   Internet

▲ Besides Earth, Io is the only planetary body in the solar system known to have active volcanoes. However, the lava from Io's volcanoes is made of sulfur, while lava on Earth is made of molten rock.

of volcanoes and fire. Although Pele and Io's other large volcanoes are not as high as the shield volcanoes of Mars, Venus, and Earth, Pele is still huge, covering an area the size of Alaska—870 miles (1,400 kilometers) across. Another volcano named Loki, after the Norse trickster god, is believed to be the most powerful volcano in the solar system. Loki produces more heat than all of Earth's active volcanoes combined.

In addition to lava flows, Io's volcanic features include lakes of liquid lava and volcanic plumes—eruptions from volcanic vents of sulfur dioxide gas that shoot up high above the surface in an umbrella-like shape. Io's thin atmosphere consists of sulfur dioxide from the erupting volcanoes and volcanic plumes. The plumes can reach as high as 310 miles (500 kilometers) above Io's surface. Sulfur dioxide powder falls like snow and blankets the ground in sulfur dioxide "frost." All of Io's surface is covered by compounds of sulfur spewed out by the volcanoes. To some people, Io looks like a pizza pie with bright yellows, oranges, reds, whites, and browns dotting the surface.

Callisto

Callisto, with a diameter of 2,995 miles (4,819 kilometers), is almost as large as the planet Mercury. It is the farthest Galilean

satellite from Jupiter, orbiting the planet at a distance of about 1.1 million miles (1.9 million kilometers). Callisto is the third largest satellite in the solar system after Ganymede and

Callisto's surface is uniformly covered with craters. It features bright areas of ice and dark areas showing highly eroded material. This moon orbits farther from Jupiter than any other Galilean moon.

Saturn's moon Titan. Callisto has a thin atmosphere of hydrogen and carbon dioxide. Scientists believe that there might be an ocean of liquid salt water, at least 6 miles (10 kilometers) deep, beneath Callisto's frozen surface. They think that this water may be the source of Callisto's weak magnetic field, which grows and shrinks in response to Jupiter's magnetic field. Below this watery layer is a mixture of rock and ice, and below it, the rocky core of Callisto.

With a surface of ice and rock that is covered with impact craters, Callisto is the most heavily cratered body in the solar system. Since there was never any volcanic activity on Callisto, most of the craters have remained intact, some for billions of years. In fact, Callisto has the oldest surface—4 billion years old—of any planet-sized object in the solar system.

The most notable feature of Callisto's surface is a ringed impact basin that looks like a huge bull's-eye. This basin, named Valhalla, is about 2,500 miles (4,000 kilometers) across, the largest impact basin of its kind in the solar system. It was probably formed when an object the size of an asteroid hit the moon's surface. There are thirteen crater chains on Callisto's surface, which were probably formed when a comet broke into pieces before striking Callisto.

Exploring Jupiter

If not for the Cold War, the intense and dangerous rivalry between the nuclear-armed United States and the former Soviet Union that lasted for most of the second half of the twentieth century, human beings still might not have ventured into outer space. Unmanned space probes might never have been sent on voyages of exploration. And all that we know today about Jupiter and the other planets in our solar system might be only what has come from observations by telescope and radio telescope. But in 1957, the Soviet Union launched an unmanned satellite named *Sputnik 1* into orbit around Earth. That launch marked the beginning of the space race between the two superpowers. That race ended on July 20, 1969. On that historic day, *Apollo 11* astronauts Neil Armstrong and Edwin "Buzz" Aldrin became the first humans to set foot on the Moon.

While the world's attention was focused on the amazing accomplishments of American astronauts and Soviet cosmonauts, both countries had begun launching unmanned space probes to the other planets. In March 1972, NASA, the National Aeronautics and Space Administration, launched *Pioneer 10,* the first attempt to reach Jupiter with a space probe.

▶ The Pioneer Missions

The *Pioneer 10* space probe sped toward Jupiter at a speed of 32,000 miles per hour (51,488 kilometers per hour). In December 1973, it flew past Jupiter at a distance of 81,000 miles (130,329 kilometers) from the planet. Scientists had wondered if the Pioneer probe would be able to pass through the Asteroid Belt

between Mars and Jupiter without being destroyed by a chunk of rock. But the probe made it safely through the region of asteroids without a problem.

When *Pioneer 10* arrived at Jupiter, it sent twenty-three low-resolution photos of the giant planet's cloud system back to Earth. Among these were photos of the Great Red Spot. *Pioneer 10* also measured the hydrogen and helium in Jupiter's atmosphere. While *Pioneer 10* was photographing Jupiter, *Pioneer 11*, which NASA had launched in April 1973, was also heading toward the planet. *Pioneer 11* reached Jupiter in December 1974, flying past the planet at a distance of 26,725 miles (43,009 kilometers). This probe sent back seventeen photos of Jupiter, including photos of the south polar region.

Pioneers 10 and *11* sent back data confirming that Jupiter has a powerful magnetic field and gives off more heat than it receives from the Sun. The data also let scientists know for sure that the planet's magnetic field is generated by electrical currents in the liquid metallic hydrogen in

NASA's Pioneer 11, *launched on* ▶ *April 5, 1973, was part of the first mission to explore the largest planet in the solar system.*

Jupiter's interior. NASA scientists were afraid that the space probes might not survive the intense radiation from Jupiter's magnetic field, but the probes were able to withstand the radiation and still transmit information back to Earth. The Pioneer probes also sent back data on temperatures and pressure within Jupiter's atmosphere. After flying past Jupiter, the Pioneer probes headed toward the outer edge of the solar system, passing other planets beyond Jupiter's orbit. When NASA scientists finally stopped tracking *Pioneer 10* in 1997, the space probe was more than 6 billion miles (9.7 billion kilometers) from Earth. It continued to send out signals until January 2003. The mission, originally designed to last twenty-one months, lasted for more than thirty years.

The Voyager Missions

Following the successful Pioneer missions, NASA in 1977 launched *Voyagers 1* and *2* to carry out additional scientific investigations of Jupiter and the other outer planets of the solar system. Although *Voyager 2* was launched first, on August 20, 1977, *Voyager 1,* taking a more direct route, reached Jupiter in March 1979. *Voyager 2* did not reach the giant planet until July 1979.

The Voyager space probes sent more than thirty-three thousand high-resolution photos back to Earth. The Voyager spacecraft were more sophisticated than the Pioneer probes and were capable of greatly improved communications. Astronomers gained an incredible wealth of new information about the Jovian system. The Voyager probes photographed Jupiter's cloud formations and storms in great detail and also sent back images of Jupiter's moons. These included photos of volcanic eruptions on the surface of Io, giant impact patterns and thirteen long chains of craters on Callisto, and evidence of flooding on Ganymede.[1] The Voyager probes discovered that Jupiter's Great Red Spot is rotating. Among other important Voyager discoveries were three new Jovian moons, auroras near Jupiter's poles, and Jupiter's faint ring system.

NASA's Voyager 1 *was launched on September 5, 1977, joining* Voyager 2, *launched earlier, on a mission to the outer planets. The images and information sent back by the Voyager probes have greatly enhanced our knowledge of Jupiter.*

After flying by Jupiter, *Voyagers 1* and *2* continued on to Saturn, sending back pictures of that planet's rings and moons. *Voyager 1* reached Saturn in November 1980, while *Voyager 2* arrived at the ringed planet in August 1981. *Voyager 1* took close-up views of Saturn's moon Titan before heading toward the edge of the solar system. *Voyager 2* skipped Titan and, following a route known as the "Grand Tour," flew by Uranus and Neptune—the first, and so far only, spacecraft to do this. *Voyager 2* reached Uranus in January 1986, discovering the planet's rings and magnetic field as well as ten moons. *Voyager 2* then reached Neptune in August 1989 and discovered that this planet, like Uranus, also has rings and a magnetic field. Both Voyager probes are now in the outermost part of the solar system, heading toward interstellar space.

The *Ulysses* Deep-Space Mission

The *Ulysses* deep-space mission, a joint effort of the European Space Agency (ESA) and NASA, was launched in 1990 to study the unexplored polar regions of the Sun. To reach its target orbit of the Sun's poles, *Ulysses* needed to use Jupiter's gravity to boost it into the correct flight path. The *Ulysses* spacecraft got its first gravity assist from Jupiter in February 1991 and its second in

February 2004. The mission is scheduled to continue until 2008, but its data from Jupiter has already given scientists a lot to be excited about.

Each time the spacecraft flew by Jupiter, an instrument on board *Ulysses* detected tiny dust particles flowing from the planet, the result of volcanic eruptions on its moon Io. These dust particles, which carry an electric charge, are influenced by Jupiter's strong magnetic field and are carried by electromagnetic forces out of Jupiter's system into space. Scientists are thrilled by these findings because they think that the dust particles coming from Jupiter are affected by magnetic forces in the same way that charged grains of dust were affected by the Sun's magnetic field in the early history of the solar system. "By studying the behaviour of these dust stream particles, we hope to gain an insight into processes that led to the formation of the moons and planets in our solar system," said Richard Marsden, the ESA's mission manager for *Ulysses*.[2]

The *Galileo* Mission

In October 1989, NASA launched the *Galileo* orbiter-probe spacecraft. *Galileo* reached Jupiter in December 1995. Its long, indirect flight path allowed it to pass close to two asteroids, called 951 Gaspra and 243 Ida. *Galileo's* images of these asteroids, the first-ever close-up photos of asteroids, revealed their irregular, elongated shapes and small craters on the surfaces. A small moon accompanying Ida was also photographed. The moon, called Dactyl, was the first known moon of an asteroid.

In July 1995, five months before the *Galileo* orbiter arrived at Jupiter, it released the bullet-shaped entry probe. The entry probe reached Jupiter in December and plunged into the Jovian atmosphere at a speed of 106,000 miles per hour (170,554 kilometers per hour). The probe penetrated Jupiter's clouds for 58 minutes to a depth of 124 miles (200 kilometers) before burning up. For the first time, scientists were able to directly sample the clouds. When the entry probe slowed to a speed of 2,000 miles per hour,

(3,218 kilometers per hour), it ejected its heat shield and opened a parachute. The probe's instruments then radioed data to the orbiter, which in turn sent the data back to the scientists on Earth. The data included readings of temperatures, pressures, wind speeds, and the makeup of the atmosphere.

The *Galileo* orbiter circled around Jupiter until September 2003. With *Galileo*'s fourteen-year mission concluded, NASA scientists sent the orbiter diving into Jupiter's atmosphere, where it disintegrated. One of the reasons that it was destroyed was to keep it from accidentally colliding with Europa, which would have contaminated that moon's surface before it could be studied for signs of life. But during its mission, *Galileo* provided more than fourteen thousand photos of the Jovian system. These included very detailed high-resolution images of the Galilean satellites, with many images of the volcanic activity on Io. The orbiter also sent back evidence of beams of electrons connecting Io to Jupiter and discovered that Ganymede has a magnetic field.

Perhaps the most amazing images from *Galileo* were received by astronomers on Earth in July 1994, when the space probe was

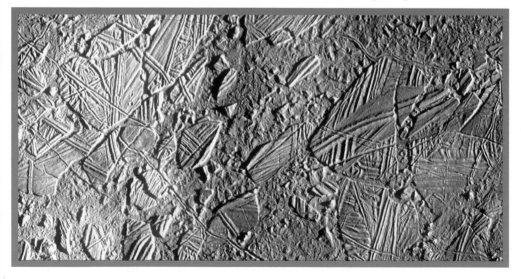

▲ The Galileo *spacecraft produced this image showing the combination of a reddish-brown surface with white and blue rafts of ice that blanket a small region of Jupiter known as Conamara.*

still about 140 million miles (225 million kilometers) from Jupiter. Because of its position at the time, the *Galileo* probe had a direct view of the collision between the comet known as Shoemaker-Levy 9 and the planet Jupiter.

The Great Collision

Astronomers believe that the Shoemaker-Levy 9 comet had been orbiting Jupiter for at least fifty years. It had come from the outer solar system and had been captured by Jupiter.[3] Then on July 7, 1992, the comet passed too close to the planet, flying by at only 12,428 miles (20,000 kilometers) from Jupiter's cloud tops. The giant planet's gravitational forces tore the comet apart. The following year, on March 23, fragments of the comet were discovered by astronomers Carolyn and Eugene Shoemaker and David Levy. The twenty fragments were lined up in a row, like a string of pearls. After careful study of their photos, Levy and the Shoemakers predicted that the comet fragments would crash into Jupiter in July 1994.

When Levy and the Shoemakers announced their discovery, astronomers all over the world trained their telescopes on the Shoemaker-Levy comet. Between July 16 and 22, 1994, the comet fragments, one by one, hit Jupiter, and the resulting fireworks were spectacular. This was the first time that human beings had ever witnessed a comet crashing into a planet. Unfortunately, the impacts happened on the night side of Jupiter, so they could not be seen directly from Earth. Scientists had to wait for Jupiter's rotation to bring the impact sites into view before the effects of the collisions could be seen.

Each fragment, possibly as large as 2 miles (3 kilometers) across, slammed into Jupiter at a speed of 134,000 miles per hour (215,606 kilometers per hour). The energy released during these impacts was equal to the simultaneous explosion of hundreds of thousands of nuclear bombs. The resulting fireballs were up to 2,500 miles (4,023 kilometers) wide. As each fragment exploded

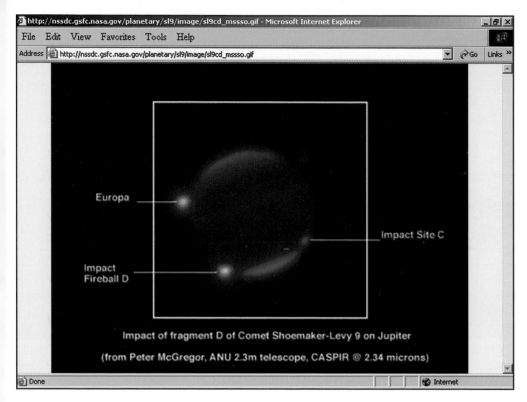

▲ This image shows where fragments C and D of the Shoemaker-Levy 9 comet smashed into Jupiter's surface.

violently in Jupiter's outer atmosphere, plumes of hot gas shot out into space as far as 2,000 miles (3,218 kilometers). Each comet fragment left a black scar twice as large as Earth. These black spots on Jupiter lasted for at least five months until they were eventually broken up by the planet's strong winds.

▶ Exploration Continues . . .

Comet Shoemaker-Levy 9's collision with Jupiter reminded astronomers that Earth had also been hit by comets and asteroids in the past, with devastating results. And of course, such collisions will probably happen again in the future. If one of the Shoemaker-Levy 9 fragments had struck Earth, it would have left

▲ *The next mission to Jupiter will be nuclear powered and even more capable than* Galileo. *Its spacecraft may look like this artist's rendition.*

a crater as large as the state of Rhode Island. There was now renewed interest in finding all of the objects in space that could someday pose a threat to Earth. As for Jupiter, all of the information obtained so far makes scientists eager to learn more about the Jovian system.

What does the future hold for missions to Jupiter? NASA plans to launch a spacecraft named *Prometheus One* in 2015 that will orbit three of Jupiter's most interesting moons: Callisto, Ganymede, and Europa.[4] If underground oceans do indeed exist beneath the surfaces of these satellites, as scientists now suspect, there may be life there as well.

Further Reading

Ashby, Ruth. *The Outer Planets.* North Mankato, Minn.: Smart Apple Media, 2003.

Asimov, Isaac, with revisions and updating by Richard Hantula. *Jupiter.* Milwaukee: Gareth Stevens Publishing, 2004.

Cole, Michael D. *Galileo Spacecraft: Mission to Jupiter.* Berkeley Heights, N.J.: Enslow Publishers, Inc., 1999.

———. *Jupiter—The Fifth Planet.* Berkeley Heights, N.J.: Enslow Publishers, Inc., 2001.

Kerrod, Robin. *Jupiter.* Minneapolis: Lerner Publications, 2000.

Koppes, Steven N. *Killer Rocks From Outer Space: Asteroids, Comets, and Meteorites.* Minneapolis: Lerner Publications, 2004.

Miller, Ron. *Extrasolar Planets.* Brookfield, Conn.: Twenty-First Century Books, 2002.

Schwabacher, Martin. *Jupiter.* Tarrytown, N.Y.: Benchmark Books, 2002.

Silverstein, Alvin, Virginia Silverstein, and Laura Silverstein Nunn. *The Universe.* Brookfield, Conn.: Twenty-First Century Books, 2003.

Simon, Seymour. *Destination Jupiter.* New York: William Morrow and Company, Inc., 2001.

Spangenburg, Ray, and Kit Moser. *A Look at Moons.* New York: Franklin Watts, 2000.

Wolverton, Mark. *The Depths of Space: The Story of the Pioneer Planetary Probes.* Washington, D.C.: Joseph Henry Press, 2004.

Chapter 1. The Biggest Planet

1. Kristin Leutwyler, *The Moons of Jupiter* (New York: W. W. Norton & Company, 2003), p. 10.

2. Ibid., p. 30.

3. Reta Beebe, *Jupiter: The Giant Planet* (Washington, D.C.: Smithsonian Institution Press, 1994), p. 11.

Chapter 2. A Giant Ball of Gas

1. Thomas R. Watters, *Planets: A Smithsonian Guide* (New York: Macmillan, 1995), p. 130.

2. David H. Levy, *Impact Jupiter: The Crash of Comet Shoemaker-Levy 9* (New York: Plenum Press, 1995), p. 72.

3. Ibid., p. 72.

Chapter 3. The Movements of Jupiter

1. Reta Beebe, *Jupiter: The Giant Planet* (Washington, D.C.: Smithsonian Institution Press, 1994), p. 24.

Chapter 4. The Jovian System

1. Kristin Leutwyler, *The Moons of Jupiter* (New York: W. W. Norton & Company, 2003), p. 218.

2. Kenneth R. Lang, *The Cambridge Guide to the Solar System* (Cambridge, England: Cambridge University Press, 2003), p. 314.

3. Ibid., p. 314.

4. Ibid., p. 303.

Chapter 5. Exploring Jupiter

1. Reta Beebe, *Jupiter: The Giant Planet* (Washington, D.C.: Smithsonian Institution Press, 1994), p. 19.

2. European Space Agency Web site, Science and Technology section, "Ulysses Sweeps Up Dust From Jupiter," February 20, 2004, <http://sci.esa.int/science-e/www/object/index.cfm?fobjectid=34713> (November 16, 2004).

3. David H. Levy, *Impact Jupiter: The Crash of Comet Shoemaker-Levy 9* (New York: Plenum Press, 1995), p. 243.

4. NASA, Solar System Exploration, Jupiter: Future Missions, "Prometheus One," n.d., <http://solarsystem.nasa.gov/missions/profile.cfm?Sort=Target&Target=Jupiter&MCode=JIMO> (November 16, 2004).

Glossary

asteroid—A rocky body in space that orbits the Sun.

Asteroid Belt—The place in our solar system between the orbits of Mars and Jupiter where most of the asteroids can be found.

eddies—Currents of water or air that move in a different direction than the main current.

geocentric theory—A theory of the universe that placed Earth at the center.

heliocentric theory—A theory of the solar system in which the Sun is at the center.

impact basin—A large crater formed by the impact of a meteorite or an asteroid.

interstellar space—The space between stars.

Jovian—Referring to Jupiter, its moons, and other features. (*Jove* is another name for the Roman god Jupiter.)

Jovian system—Jupiter and its moons and rings.

magnetic field—A region of space near a magnetized body, such as a planet, where magnetic forces can be detected.

magnetosphere—The region that makes up a planet's magnetic field.

spectrometer—An instrument connected to a telescope that separates light into different wavelengths, producing a spectrum, or series of colored bands that is formed when light is broken up.

stripes—Dark and light bands of clouds in Jupiter's atmosphere.

velocity—The rate of motion, or speed.